Alpacas

by Julie Murray

Abdo Kids Jumbo is an Imprint of Abdo Kids
abdobooks.com

abdobooks.com

Published by Abdo Kids, a division of ABDO, P.O. Box 398166, Minneapolis, Minnesota 55439.

Printed in the United States of America, North Mankato, Minnesota.

052025

092025

Photo Credits: Adobe Stock, Alamy, Getty Images, Shutterstock

Production Contributors: Teddy Borth, Jennie Forsberg, Grace Hansen
Design Contributors: Candice Keimig, Pakou Moua

Library of Congress Control Number: 2024947616

Publisher's Cataloging-in-Publication Data

Names: Murray, Julie, author.

Title: Alpacas / by Julie Murray

Description: Minneapolis, Minnesota : Abdo Kids, 2026 | Series: Fancy farm animals | Includes online resources and index.

Identifiers: ISBN 9798384905219 (lib. bdg.) | ISBN 9798384905912 (ebook) | ISBN 9798384906261 (Read-to-me ebook)

Subjects: LCSH: Alpaca--Juvenile literature. | Farm animals--Juvenile literature. | Livestock--Juvenile literature. | Domestic animals--Juvenile literature.

Classification: DDC 636.3--dc23

Table of Contents

Alpacas

Alpacas are known for their soft **fleece**. They are cute and friendly! They are popular fancy farm animals.

Alpacas were **domesticated** 6,000 years ago by the **Inca**. They lived high in the Andes Mountains. There are no wild alpacas today. Many are found on farms and ranches around the world.

South
America
Andes
Mountains
N
W
E
S

There are two kinds of alpacas. The Huacaya alpaca is the most common. It has thick, fluffy **fleece**. The Suri alpaca has long, silky fleece.

Suri
alpaca
Huacaya
alpaca

Alpacas communicate in many ways. They hum when they are happy. They scream or spit when they are scared. They also spit when they are angry.

Body

Alpacas stand up to 6 feet (1.8 m) tall from head to toe. They weigh between 100 and 200 pounds (45-91 kg). Males are larger than females.

Alpacas have a long neck and long legs. They have a small head and pointy ears. Their body is covered in **fleece**. Their fleece can be many different colors.

Alpacas are raised for their **fleece**. They are **sheared** once a year. Each alpaca gives about 5 to 10 pounds (2.3-4.5 kg) of fleece each shearing. The fleece is used to make blankets, clothes, and yarn.

Diet

Alpacas are **grazing** animals. They mainly eat grass and hay. They enjoy foods such as apples and carrots too. They eat 2 to 4 pounds (0.9 to 1.8 kg) of food each day.

Baby Alpacas

Baby alpacas are called cria. Females give birth to one cria at a time. It weighs 18 pounds (8.2 kg) at birth. It drinks its mother's milk for six months.

More Facts

- Alpacas are social animals. They need to live in a herd. This makes them feel safe and happy.

- Alpacas are related to camels and llamas.

Camel

- Instead of hooves, alpacas have soft padded feet. They do not disturb the grass and land where they **graze**.

Glossary

domesticated – made useful to humans and living near them rather than in the wild.

fleece – the wool of an animal, usually a sheep.

graze – to feed on growing grass.

Inca – an ancient group of people that ruled Peru.

shear – to trim the fleece or hair from something.

Index